Resting on a Pillow of Prayers

Poems of Loss, Hope, and Healing

God's blessings,
Jennifer

Jennifer Fisch Lemp

ISBN 979-8-88851-680-5 (Paperback)
ISBN 979-8-88851-681-2 (Digital)

Copyright © 2023 Jennifer Fisch Lemp
All rights reserved
First Edition

All rights reserved. No part of this publication may be reproduced, distributed, or transmitted in any form or by any means, including photocopying, recording, or other electronic or mechanical methods without the prior written permission of the publisher. For permission requests, solicit the publisher via the address below.

Covenant Books
11661 Hwy 707
Murrells Inlet, SC 29576
www.covenantbooks.com

This book is gratefully dedicated to my husband, George, who has loved me through every season of our lives together and has always believed in me and in us.

This one's for you, sweetheart, with all my love.

Contents

Introduction vii

Poems of Hope 1
Poems of Suffering 11
Poems of Loss 25
Poems of Recovery 35
Poems of Forgiveness 45
Poems of Love 57
Poems of Grace 69
Poems of Faith 81
Poems of Mission 93

Introduction

Suffering is the greatest treasure on earth; it purifies the soul.
—The Diary of Saint Maria Faustina
Kowalska: Divine Mercy in My Soul

Years ago, I did not believe this statement. I thought that suffering was to be avoided at all costs. Now I know differently. Experiencing an eating addiction and recovery, the loss of my brother and parents, and my diagnosis of recurrent cancer catapulted me into a long period of questioning and, ultimately, reaffirming my faith in God. The suffering that these events caused drew me closer to God and to the peace that I found only He can give. I started writing poems to ease my pain and discovered that they comforted me and others in a profound way and did, indeed, bring peace, hope, and joy.

I pray that these poems will do the same for you.

Poems of Hope

For I know well the plans I have in mind for you—
oracle of the Lord—plans for your welfare and not
for woe, so as to give you a future of hope.
—Jeremiah 29:11 (NABRE)

Sweet Slumber

I'm resting on a pillow of prayers
Soft and wide and deep,
Lifting me to God on high
In waking and in sleep.

Each feather is a fervent prayer
From every loving heart
That holds me body, mind, and soul
As God does do His part.

I can lie down with no fear
Of what is to come
Because I know, in life or death,
The feather prayers will keep me warm.

Hope

Hope lifts its weary head
To find
Another day,
Another climb.

Gazing upward
On its knees
It sees
The possibilities,

Illumined by the One
Who knows
What to give
And to withhold.

Joy

A glimpse, a glance,
To see, by chance,
The beauty of
The heavenly expanse.

Unseen, unheard,
In skies above,
Throng saints and angels
In eternal love.

The Journey

With faith we see beyond the pain,
The drear, the sadness, and the rain;
If we but look upon the Cross
Nothing in life will we count as loss.

Each day a gift,
A new surprise
To make us strong
And meek and wise.

Nothing wasted in His plan
To get us to the promised land;
Each small event, so often missed,
Is always meant to us assist.

Safe Harbor

My compass is the Cross,
You see,
For life's journey
It will always be.

Guiding me
Without fail,
No matter where
My ship may sail,

Showing me
That for all time
Both love and sacrifice
Must be mine.

Though I be far from home
And lost,
Adrift, directionless
And tossed,

He rights my ship
And draws me back,
His love, the magnet
Keeping me on track.

Jesus

Our hope resides
In Him alone,
Who, for our sins,
Did atone.

There is no other
Sister or brother
Who loves us more
And did us restore.

Now is our chance
To serve and adore
Until we meet
On heaven's shore.

My Hope

In the midst of all my grief
I sense a Presence still and deep.
He is there, in my boat,
To row me safely and keep me afloat.

I will not sink with Him on board,
He is the One I know as Lord.
More powerful than the greatest storm,
He sees me through to each new morn.

No matter what the future holds,
In His heart I will repose.
I am His and He is mine
For then, for now, and for all time.

Poems of Suffering

The God of all grace Who called you to His eternal glory in Christ [Jesus] will Himself restore, confirm, strengthen, and establish you after you have suffered a little.
—1 Peter 5:10 (NABRE)

Suffering

The greatest teacher
I have known
With silence taught
And preached a tome.

Without a word
It spoke to me;
Its truth was harsh
And would not let me be.

It held on tight
Despite my fight
Until I finally came to see
Acceptance was the golden key.

Then, at last, I understood,
The One who made a gift of it
For love to save all sinners would
Accept it back and turn it into good.

My Fervent Plea

Remove the beast
And let me be
At peace,
At home with my family.

The healing pain
Will lay me low
To teach me patience
And that You are in control.

Let me trust Your goodness,
Your mercy, and Your might
To heal me completely
As I do fight the fight.

Doubt

A saboteur
In shadows lurks,
Stalking you
In all your works.

No trust in self
Or others too,
Little joy
In all you do.

Time to believe and renew
The convictions true
That inspired you
And gave comfort too.

The Valley

I want to hide,
I want to flee
From the grief
Surrounding me.

Pain of body,
Pain of mind,
No escape
Do I find.

But it's *through* the valley,
Not around,
That my Shepherd
Will ever be found.

My Suffering

Your gift,
A cross,
To bear for You.

The weight
You place on me,
It's true.

Sweet burden borne in love renewed
Earns for me
Forever with You.

The cross exchanged
For the crown,
Which remains.

Fear

Fear does grip
With its viselike hold,
Imprisoning spirit,
Body, mind, and soul.

Unable to move
Or think, or feel,
The sense of dread
Is far too real.

I want to break free
But don't have the key;
It resides in Him
Who conquered sin.

Knowing I'm forgiven,
Loved, and cherished
Lets me believe
That I will not perish.

The vessel of trust
Is an absolute must
To banish this foe
And let His love flow.

"Where love abounds
No fear is found";
Instead, there is peace
That will not cease.

To Suffer

Escape from pain
Not meant to be,
Not on earth
For you or me,

But only
In eternity,
And no longer
A mystery!

Courage

To live in Him
And accept
That what He sends
Is for the best.

Going forth
Despite our fear,
Trusting Him
To be near.

Suffering
As He once did,
His mother too,
That we might live.

Their chain of sacrifice we complete,
Our sorrow and theirs do meet
In every bead, faith, hope, and love
Linking us to heaven above.

Service

To let go of myself,
And not cling so tightly,
Trust and be free
And then give so rightly.

To give is to suffer,
To empty, to bow
Before God and man
To serve them now.

Let me follow Your heart
In all that I do,
To please and honor
And always be true.

The Fall

The lot of us
Who fell from grace,
Who disobeyed
And now run the race.

The pain, the trials
Great and small,
Proving character
Once, for all.

Praying, weeping,
Laughing, sleeping,
All in life
In God's good keeping.

Sacrifice

I cling to You
In doubt and pain,
Praying for relief,
But offering it as gain.

Suffering as You once did
For sinners poor
That we might live
Forevermore.

Dying and rising,
The endless round,
Sorrow and joy
Are where You are found.

Poems of Loss

Blessed are they who mourn, for they will be comforted.
—Matthew 5:4 (NABRE)

Goodbye

Silent halls,
Silent walls,
Only the photos
That to us call.

The rooms that rang
With loving voices
Have gone to sleep
And no one rejoices.

Still in our hearts
Forevermore,
But not their faces
At our door.

Kaleidoscope

It's a watercolor moment,
Going back in time,
Remembering those visions
Of warmth and calm and charm.

A watery mosaic,
Blended colors of my life,
Shimmering expectantly,
Untouched by human strife.

Legacy

Our lives, on loan
To us on earth;
Our souls, forever
In rebirth.

Once here, then gone,
We leave echoes of our songs
That others hear
Their whole lives long.

So learn your song, sing it loud and clear,
Without pretense and without fear,
Knowing that all tunes sweet
Are only learned at the Master's feet.

Farewell

I'm gone,
I'm free,
Don't weep for me;
At last, the peace of eternity!

Earth's woes and troubles
Far behind,
A distant memory
In my new mind.

A place prepared
By the King
With just what I need,
To be with Him.

Life to Life

Sagging spirit,
Sagging mind,
Body worn out,
Not much time.

The bridge to cross
And leave behind
Those you love
So dear and kind.

The One who sees
And knows all things
Will take you home
And over you sing,

"Enter your rest,
You've done your best,
You've loved Me true,
And others too.

You leave your dear ones here on earth,
But you will have a new rebirth!
Those gone before will rejoice to see you,
Welcome you home and never leave you."

Longing

I remember the times,
They're etched in my mind,
Seeing this mother and her daughter of nine,
Just sharing time.

The tears rise,
To my surprise,
I'm reliving the days
With the girls I prize.

All those times,
Thinking they would last,
That they would never pass,
At least not so fast.

Time now,
So short,
Sharing a meal, a movie, a text;
What should I expect?

My heart not wanting to close,
Not wanting to impose,
So I sit and doze
And remember…

Absent

Lord, help me to see
That it's all right to be
Angry and sad,
And feeling so bad.

A woman so dear
Will never be near;
My best friend is gone,
The one I counted upon.

Although I can't see,
I know she will be
Praying for me
And our family.

Silence and sleep,
So very deep,
Allow me to heal
As Your love is revealed.

Poems of Recovery

For God is the one Who, for His good purpose,
works in you both to desire and to work.
—Philippians 2:13 (NABRE)

To Free the Butterfly

Around my mind and heart, as well,
Was spun a hard, protective shell;
Built by years of doubt and fear,
Especially as others did draw near.

This chrysalis of my defense
Kept me safe, it made sense;
But inside, in the dark,
I longed for light, and warmth, and flight.

At long last, the day, it came,
To emerge, despite the pain,
To take my place in the human race
With thanks to God for His saving grace.

Release

My body encircled
By a bandage of flesh
To protect against wounds
That seem to stay fresh.

A cushion to soften
The hard edges of life,
It never resolves
The inner strife.

Only through shedding
The unhealthy cocoon
Can I break free
And shoot for the moon!

Recovery

To face the truth,
At last to be
With others who
Can understand me.

I hurt, I long,
I strive to belong,
While knowing, full well,
I have been in the wrong.

The choices I've made
Were not at all free;
My eating addiction
Has been enslaving me.

The food that gives life
Has come to mean death,
The death of my choice
To be my best.

I'm ready to start,
I'm ready to change,
I'm ready to accept help
To not stay the same.

The Emptying

Clearing my house
Inside and out,
Not only from that which you see,
But from the deeper recesses of me.

Letting go and becoming free,
This is a new experience for me;
Peace and joy are showing their faces,
All a part of God's generous graces.

Falling

The depth of my pain,
Back again
In a flood of regret
And fear, and shame.

Just when I think all is well
The sadness swells,
The urge surges back, and I succumb
For the courage I lack.

Relapse

I've reached the end,
Yet again,
Of my strength
To not give in.

When will I learn
That all is lost
Unless I go
To the Cross?

If I take it up
Every day
I can be abstinent
If I go His way.

Comfort

Not in a bottle,
Not in a bite,
Not in a song
Or a beautiful sight.

Only within
Where He dwells
Can true peace be found
As He calms fears that swell.

At Any Time

At any time
The Tempter can strike,
Luring us
To take that bite.

As in Eden, long ago,
It starts us on the path of woe;
Paul knew it well, as all mortals too,
We do what we don't want to do.

How to resist and stand our ground?
Admit that only God wears the crown.
Use the tools, day after day,
To avoid becoming Satan's prey.

Poems of Forgiveness

[And] be kind to one another, compassionate, forgiving
one another as God has forgiven you in Christ.
—Ephesians 4:32 (NABRE)

Tempest-Tossed

Across the waters of my soul
A raging wind did blow and blow,
Holding hostage every drop
Of heedless wave, under key and lock.

Mercy to calm the choppy sea
Had become an enemy;
It wasn't fair, it wasn't just,
To have to endure this breach of trust.

Hurts clutched to the heart
Yearned to break free
And give me peace,
And just let me be.

And I, full blind
As I fought to be,
Closed my eyes
And played make-believe.

I refused to change,
Refused to grow,
Refused to forgive
And so consigned myself to woe.

Until, at last,
Long ignored,
The voice of God
Cut through the roar.

I finally did yield
And loosened my grip;
The betrayal of others
I did let slip.

Forgive and forget
Was finally in place,
And only, I knew,
By His merciful grace.

My murky life,
Now clear to see,
God took me to His Son,
Hanging on a tree.

The Father's Plea

I am weeping tears of rain
To wash away your guilt and shame.
Another year, another chance,
Come to Me, and join the dance.

Put fear behind you,
Step out and see
My Son does shine
When you repent and believe.

Letting Go

I used to count them,
One by one,
Those pains and hurts
That were never undone.

And now I find
I live above,
Detached from all
But His great love.

In body, soul, and spirit free
I can release
What was, what is,
And what will be.

Forgiven

Driven by pain,
By fear and by shame,
I overdo,
It's nothing new.

Trying to numb
The feelings of doubt
That I don't deserve
And must do without.

Needing to prove
I am worthy to be
Saved and redeemed
Is hurting me.

Accepting His mercy
With a thankful heart
Will enable me
To make a new start.

Confession

He shines a light inside my mind
Exposing sin too dark to find.

Accepts my sorrow and my shame,
Reminding me that's why He came.

He opens His heart and lets me in,
His blood to wash away my sin.

Come to Me

Saint and sinner,
One and the same,
Saved by God's grace,
Called by name.

Despite our sin
He uses us
To witness to Him
And bear His Cross.

All He asks
Is a willing heart,
Ready to give
And make a new start.

Forgiveness

Trust the Truth
Who set you free,
Who gave Himself
Upon a tree.

Look to Him
In times of woe
And gather strength
To love the foe.

In the end
All is dust,
Except our souls,
Which we pray are just.

Let it go,
Your pain and grief,
To Him who promised
Blessed relief.

Freedom

Forgive and forget,
No time to fret,
Let go the ego
And the darkness will follow.

Open your heart,
Receive His light
Let it warm your soul
And give it flight.

Poems of Love

Beloved, let us love one another, because love is of God; everyone who loves is begotten by God and knows God.
—1 John 4:7 (NABRE)

Together Forever

Blessed be the tie that binds
Two hearts in endless love,
Woven with deft angel hands
And joined to heaven above.

Not two, but Three, joined in harmony,
The tie not seen, but felt,
The One who made you stays with you
And leads you to Himself.

Friendship

When things are real
And talk is plain,
With no pretense
Or fear or shame.

Unmeasured words
From heart to heart
Flowing easily
Until dark.

Giving spirits,
True concern,
Each for the other,
Turn after turn.

Our Love

The long, still notes
Only we can hear
Keep us together
Through the years.

Me high, you low,
Alone in our parts,
But forever together
In our harmony of hearts.

Listen

Listen to the silence,
It has much to tell
Of dreams forgotten
That made the heart swell.

The Family Meal

Come to the table,
Come without fear,
Laughter and tears
Are both welcome here.

Come to the table,
No pretense allowed,
Bring only yourself
Unplugged, in the here and now.

Tell your story
For all to hear,
Listen and ponder
With hearts as ears.

Renew and refresh,
Sharing as one
Food with each other,
The meal never to be done…

She and He

The years were kind to her frame,
And her womanly curves
Remained the same
And called his name.

Her smile warmed his heart,
With joy to impart,
For their love had retained
Its original spark.

Inheritance

Born in love,
Formed in faith,
We grew up
With Your grace.

Now we see the fruits of love
Our parents gave
To make us strong,
To make us brave.

Rooted in You
They toiled to teach
How to live
From what You preached.

Heart of My Heart

Heart of my heart,
Love of my life,
My only one,
Never depart.

Mom, My First Love

Twinkling eyes
Full of wonder and surprise,
Memories of kisses
From days gone by.

She taught me well
And loved me more,
Sacrificed much
So that I could soar.

Giving the best
From her heart,
Loving her God
And doing her part.

Poems of Grace

For by grace you have been saved through faith, and this is not from you; it is the gift of God; it is not from works, so no one may boast.
—Ephesians 2:8–9 (NABRE)

The Room

I'm in a room
Inside myself
Where only
I can go.

The light streams in,
It's warm and bright,
With colors
All aglow.

He sits with me
And comforts me
As only
He can do.

Reminding me
Of His great love
And that He will
See me through.

The Dwelling

You build in me a house of love
To shelter friend and foe,
Where angels light the rooms at night
And in daytime shine and glow.

On the top floor lives my mind and will,
On the next my heart and soul,
And on the ground floor live my hands raised up
With service as their goal.

The strength within my walls comes first
From a love of Thee,
And then, from love of neighbor
Shown in hospitality.

Peace

You light my days
With rays of love,
Care and comfort
From above.

Filling me
With an inner glow
That warms my soul
And makes me whole.

In the darkness
When I cry
You rescue me
And draw me nigh.

Reminding me
That all is well,
Since You are God
And in me do dwell.

Rescuer

I close my eyes
And recall
All the times
I did not fall.

Upheld by You,
So faithful and true,
Throughout the years,
Despite my fears.

Why do I doubt
What You're about
When, in the end,
It's my good You intend?

The proof is there,
And ample too,
You hold me close
And see me through.

Only You

When all is said
And all is done,
We turn to You,
The Holy One.

Refresh our souls,
Light our minds,
That we may, You,
Our Love, to find.

The Treasure

I met my King today,
He Who my debt did pay;
Hidden in a host
With the Father and the Holy Ghost.

The Giver and the Gift combined
Shares Himself as bread and wine;
Sparing nothing, His heart divine,
Pure love, holy and sublime.

The Gift

The pain that turns my eyes to You,
Away from self, and to what's true.
Do not delay, my soul,
Return to the One who makes you whole.

My Desire

Your Spirit enfolds me,
Holds me,
Molds me,
Makes me Your own.

I long for You,
Pine for You,
Thirst for You,
Wait for You alone, my God.

True Peace

Be still, my heart,
And look within,
Find Jesus there,
Know Him as friend.

Midst trial and woe,
Through pain and loss
He stands with me
And bears my cross.

He teaches me
To trust in Him,
His grace to fill me
To the brim.

Poems of Faith

We know all things work for good for those who love
God, who are called according to His purpose.
—Romans 8:28 (NABRE)

Faith

I'm living on miracles,
Riding the tide,
Handing it over,
He will provide.

I do not see
What He has in store,
But I know my Maker,
My Savior, my Lord.

I'm letting Him lead me,
Love me, and more,
Trusting His promises
Given before.

He says,
"I'll stay in your boat
And keep you afloat,
Not let you drown,
My mercies abound.

Just pray with your heart,
Your mind and your soul,
My power protects you,
And I am your goal.

You can believe
I do hear your voice
And answer your pleas
So that you may rejoice.

Know, My child,
You are never forsaken,
I want you to learn
From what I have taken.

Just watch and wait,
I am never late,
My will is unfolding,
Your life I am holding.

I'll show you what matters,
Your dreams, they may shatter,
But know, in the end,
It's your good I intend."

To Believe

To let go
Of all the pain,
And to breathe,
Relaxed again.

To detach from what has been
And what will be,
And focus my eyes
On the Mystery.

To accept
Without knowledge or sight,
Simply because
I trust the Light.

The test of faith
Before me lies
From the One who can,
And does, know why.

Sovereign

The Master gives,
The Master takes,
And all He does
Is for our sakes.

Then trust I must
If I am to be
The servant true
He expects of me.

I give myself
To Him alone,
Obeying His Word
To reach my heavenly home.

Trials

I find my strength within Your will,
It stands before me to be fulfilled;
You send it from Your loving heart
With countless graces to impart.

Grant that I will only want
That which You decree,
The yoke You place upon my back,
Which fits me perfectly.

Through pain and sorrow, joy and peace,
You remain the same,
Sustaining me with Your very Self,
Again and again and again.

When I am sad or mad or glad
It makes no difference to You,
You only want my loving heart
To pour Your mercy into.

Sustain in me a willing spirit,
Strong and meek and free,
And let me see with the eyes of faith
Your eternal, sovereign majesty.

In His Will

In His will my peace is found
And oft my plans
All come unwound
Without a sound.

Wisdom and grace
He showers from above,
Drenching me
With His eternal love.

My destiny is in His hands;
He reveals to me a more perfect plan
To journey to Him
And the promised land.

I must but obey
And behold
His merciful power
And glory unfold.

The Good Fight

Trusting His love,
The only way
To do His will,
Day by day.

Listening to His voice
In the middle of the night,
Praying for courage
To do what's right.

Dying to self,
And living for Him,
The constant battle
It has always been.

But through His grace
So freely given
I can obey
And so, reach heaven.

The Offering

Lose the fear,
Live by faith,
Come to Me,
I give you grace.

Not just for you,
For others too,
Who watch and see
How you serve Me.

Be a sign
Of love divine
And suffer well
With praise to tell.

Night

The day is done
And so am I,
My body, mind, and spirit dry.

All poured out
In countless ways,
It's time for me to kneel and pray.

Final Journey

I take His hand,
Not wanting to start,
But He draws me close
To His merciful heart.

Walking with Him
To protect and guide
On the journey
To the other side…

Poems of Mission

He said to them, "Go into the world and
proclaim the Gospel to every creature."
—Mark 16:15 (NABRE)

A New Year Melody

As daylight breaks
And we rise
A song descends
From the skies.

Listen now
And you will hear
A tune so sweet
For the New Year.

The joy of life,
A new day,
The chance to live,
To give, and obey.

A moment to pause
And close our eyes,
Offer Him our year
And pray we thrive.

Putting Him first,
Ahead of the rest,
Why would we hesitate
And forgo the best?

"Come to Me,"
He begs us to do;
His merciful heart burns
For me and for you.

Nowhere else
Will we find
True love, true joy,
True peace of mind.

In His will
We will discover
The marvels He leads us
To uncover.

The Greatest Gift

The greatest gift
We've been given
Is the means
To reach heaven.

He died for us
Out of love;
He wants us all
To join Him above.

He tells us how
In His Book;
Spend some time
And take a look!

He spells it out
In great detail,
How to love and how to live,
How to serve and how to forgive.

We sinners all need His grace,
His Word, His Body, to run the race;
Only through the church He gave
Can we live and be saved.

To be with Him,
Our free choice,
He invites us all,
Respond to His voice!

Confess your sins
And be healed,
Then your path in life
Will be revealed.

On the narrow road
Take His hand;
It is the only way
To the promised land.

Transfigure Me

In disguise
On the Cross,
My King and my God,
For me, You suffered loss.

Change my heart
And let
Me see
Your eternal majesty.

Draw me closer
Day by day
To Your light,
To Your way.

Let me leave
My sin behind
And cling to You,
The one, true Vine.

Give me courage
To face the truth,
With You at my side
To forgive and soothe.

Grant me the grace
To be pure,
To love You first
And to endure.

Align my will
With Yours alone,
To serve You well
And to atone.

Sacred Art

The truths of our faith,
In timeless hues,
Captured forever,
Our souls to infuse.

Mosaics and paintings
Recall the life
Of our Lord and Savior
And His great strife.

Sculpted angels,
Saints and popes
Show us the way
To fulfill all hopes.

Christ's true church
On mission today
To save all mankind
From death and decay.

Invitation

We've heard His Word,
We know it by heart;
He died to redeem us,
We must do our part.

Don't waste your time
In idle pursuits
That do little good
For others or you.

Humble yourself,
Get back on the path
To life, not death,
And avoid His wrath.

He shows you the way
It is narrow and straight,
Accept His mercy,
It is never too late.

He is the Master
Who made us all,
Without His guidance
We stumble and fall.

So suffer for good
To be worthy of heaven;
Avoid the bad
That will lead you to ruin.

Give Him your life,
Every piece of your soul,
It's already His,
And He is your goal.

One way or the other
It's always a choice;
He's calling to you
Will you hear His voice?

Wisdom

Those who upon Him do gaze
Bow their heads and give Him praise,
Thank Him for the graces given
To obey and so reach heaven.

Time and treasures
Humbly spent,
The world laughs now,
But will later lament.

The Lord of Life asks nothing less
Than the beating heart inside each breast
To turn to Him
And be ever blest.

Our total gift,
Pure and fine,
Returning the love
Of that Love Divine.

We join our fellow saints here and above,
United in His eternal love,
In blessed communion forevermore,
Whether on earth, in fire, or on heaven's shore.

Vocation

To hear what is not spoken,
To listen with a silent soul,
To hearken to the voice of God
Revealing your true role.

God Calling

Take the plunge
And risk it all,
Trust the Master
And answer His call.

Open your heart,
Let His love show,
Sharing His light
To warm friend and foe.

My Plea

With all my sins
And all my faults,
I praise You, Lord,
For You are God.

Love, Beauty, Truth,
Life, Goodness, and Being,
All that I will ever need
In this life and in heaven.

Comfort me, dear Lord,
And let me see
In clarity of mind and heart
Your eternal majesty.

Fill me with
That inner peace
That You did promise
Would not cease.

Love me, Lord,
As only You are able,
And feed me, Lord,
From Your blessed table.

Promised Land

Get in the boat,
No time to waste,
Glory-bound and overflowing,
God's kingdom awaits!

No time to look back,
No time for regrets,
Just focus on Jesus,
He'll do the rest.

Repent and be healed,
Cleansed to the core,
A new life awaits
With oh, so much more!

Joy everlasting,
God to behold,
With all our loved ones
Forevermore…

A Truly Blessed Life

Not riches or gold
Or not growing old,

Not worldly pleasure
Or only life's leisure,

Not focus on self
And nobody else.

But a heart that is true
To the Master of you,

A will that obeys
Every word that He says,

A spirit refreshed
To give Him your best,

A mind filled with Him
And not silly whims,

A mouth that says,
"I'll go where I'm led,"

A voice lifting praise
To the Power Who saves,

A hand to the poor
To open the door,

Eyes of compassion
Watching *His* Passion,

A welcoming glance
To give others a chance,

A vision so true
As if God's looking out through you,

Ears open wide
To hear those outside,

A head bent in prayer,
With some time spent there,

A trust that finds peace
Where all fear shall cease,

Faith to *step* up
And not to *give* up,

Hope that inspires
And sets you on fire,

Love with its root
As Jesse's Blessed Shoot,

Power that's found
In laying your life down,

Eternal life
After the strife,

A crown of glory
Where all is holy,

Seeing Him face-to-face
After the race,

Living with Love
And all others above,

Forever and ever…

About the Author

Jennifer Fisch Lemp was raised in California and Texas and grew up in the church. An avid wordsmith like her father, she has always found contentment in the sound and meaning of words, as reflected in her poetry.

Jennifer remains active in her church and never imagined that her faith in God would be put to the test as fiercely as it has been. In the past nine years, she lost her brother, her niece, both her parents, and her husband's parents. In 2018, Jennifer was diagnosed with an aggressive, recurrent form of cancer. Since then, she has endured four major surgeries and four different courses of chemotherapy. At first, Jennifer thought that the cancer was a punishment from God. However, over time, she came to realize that it was really a gift from God since it drew her closer to Him and opened her eyes in a new way to His grace and blessings.

In His goodness and mercy, God prepared Jennifer for her cancer journey by giving her coping tools the year before her cancer diagnosis. She worked the Twelve Steps of Recovery through HOW-Overeaters Anonymous and released a significant amount of both physical and emotional weight.

Writing poetry is Jennifer's way of coming to terms with her losses in light of God's promises. Her life experiences inspire the poetry that she hopes will comfort her readers and give them peace. She remains grateful to God for the countless blessings He continues to shower upon her.

Jennifer loves spending time with her husband, George, and traveling to visit her daughters, sons-in-law, and grandchildren. She currently resides with her husband in the beautiful wine country of California and, when able to do so, enjoys hiking, biking, and trips to the ocean.

Printed in the USA
CPSIA information can be obtained
at www.ICGtesting.com
LVHW041446081023
760406LV00002BA/6